Making Wonderful Cards for Christmas

Tips to Make DIY Christmas Card

© 2020 All rights reserved

Table of Content

INTRODUCTION	3
STAMPED CHRISTMAS GREETING CARDS	4
STRING ART CHRISTMAS CARDS	9
REINDEER CHRISTMAS CARD	15
CHRISTMAS TREE SHADOW BOX CARD	20
MAKE PAINT CHIP CHRISTMAS CARDS	29

Introduction

Christmas comes but once a year, and it's time to spread that festive cheer. So design a card, it isn't hard, and show them all you care.

Christmas cards have a very distinct design language and vocabulary that sees images of reindeers, trees, snow and Santa accompanied by words such as 'joy,' 'peace,' 'merry' and 'happy' topped off with a color palette of green, red and gold. But there's no reason you can't be creative within this framework or experimental outside of it while still expressing the sentiment of Christmas.

So no matter who the recipient is – whether it's customers and clients or friends and family – here are stunning Christmas cards that will have you decking the halls and singing joy to the world.

Stamped Christmas greeting Cards

It's always nice to send and receive "real" greetings cards, the virtual ones are sweet too but I do prefer the traditional paper ones! Don't do agree with me? So here is an easy idea to make your own stamped greetings cards. It's very simple to make and your friends and family will surely appreciate the handmade touch.

Materials

- A foam sheet
- A cutter
- A pencil
- A piece of cardboard
- A foam brush
- Paint
- Cardstock paper

Instructions

Step 1:

Take the foam sheet and cut a rectangle of 4×6, which is the standard size for a greeting card. Draw your pattern on it. Remember you will have to cut out the shapes so try first with a simple design. I made some Christmas trees and stars.

Step 2:

Using your craft knife, cut the shapes out. Don't make to small shapes as the paint will stick in it and won't appear when stamping.

Step 3:

Glue a piece of cardboard on the back of the foam, with a glue gun for example. This will give your stamp a sturdy backdrop and will help you to apply it easily on the paper sheet. With a brush or a sponge brush put paint on the foam stamp. Be sure to spread the paint everywhere, then apply the stamp on the paper and press to ensure that of the surface is well stamped on the paper.

Step 4:

You can apply the stamp directly on your greeting card. In this case you will need a sheet of paper of 5×17 than you will fold in the middle. You will apply the stamp on the front part of your card.

Or you can stamp on a white cardstock and once the paint is dry cut it out and glue it on a colored sheet of 5×17 folded in half.

Whatever option you choose, I suggest you to make a few try on plain paper to see how your stamp works.

Enjoy!

STRING ART CHRISTMAS CARDS

Make festive **Christmas cards** with the kids with this easy string art tutorial. Kids will love threading yarn and beads through to make trees. You can also make holiday shapes, like a pretty angel card.

Materials

- **Yarn**
- Large needle
- Cardstock
- **Beads**
- Small piece of silver pipe cleaner (for the angel)
- Glue
- Felt
- Pencil
- Letter stamp set (optinal)

Instructions

Step 1. Cut your cardstock into card size shapes. Trace a holiday shape like a tree or angel onto the card with a pencil. You can freehand the shapes or look up clipart online to cut out and use as a template.

Step 2. Poke holes with your needle along your drawn shape and erase the pencil lines. Start threading yarn through the holes, making sure to tie a knot on your first go through so it stays secure in the back of the card. Note: we added a beaded star to the top which is optional.

Step 3. Continue stringing and then start adding the beads. Continue stringing until your tree looks full.

Step 4. You can also add stamped letters as we did.

Step 5. The back of the card will look "stringy" so you can cut a piece of felt and glue on the back of the card to cover any imperfections.

Repeat the same process for the angel. Instead of beads, we glued a small piece of silver pipe cleaner as the halo.

Good luck!

Reindeer Christmas Card

Rudolph the reindeer is one of our favorite Christmas characters, so we are kicking off this years collection of cards with the simplest ever reindeer Christmas card for kids to make! Just a few cuts and a bit of glue and you'll have the nicest looking Christmas card ever!

Ready? Let's make one!

Materials

- A thumb or finger
- Brown paint (or red, yellow and blue if you'll be mixing your own)
- White paint or white gel pen
- Glue
- Red felt for the nose – but you can use any material or paper you have laying around
- Black fineliner
- Piece of card

Instructions

1. Mix up your paint

If you've bought brown paint then you're good to go. If not, you can make brown by mixing red, blue and yellow.

I prefer to mix my own because the reindeer face will be made from varying shades of brown rather than being flat colour.

2. Print your reindeer face
Stick your thumb in the paint and press it down firmly on card. It doesn't matter if it's not perfect, your reindeer will have more character!

3. Cut out the nose
I've used red felt for the nose but you can use any fabric or paper you have to hand.

Glue the nose to the bottom of the thumb print.

4. Give your reindeer some eyes
Put two small blobs of white paint onto the face and allow to dry. Once the paint is dry draw on some eyeballs. Don't worry if you're reindeer looks a bit boss-eyed, tis the season to be merry!

5. Draw on the details
Use a fineliner to give your reindeer some personality. Add some antlers and accessories such as a scarf.

6. Fold card
Fold your card in half or cut out your reindeer to make gift tags.

Ta dah!

CHRISTMAS TREE SHADOW BOX CARD

Materials

- 65 lb. cardstock (I used red, dark red, green, blue, yellow, and white)
- Tacky glue
- Spray adhesive
- Scoring stylus (if you're using a Cricut)
- Cricut pen (if you're using a Cricut)
- A way to cut out the pattern in the cardstock (I used a **Cricut**)

Instructions

Step 1:

First, cut out all of your cardstock pieces. This shadow box card is a bit more complicated as two colors are revealed when the pull tab slides up, and thus there are more pieces and a bit more complexity to the cut.

Step 2:

Once everything is cut out, begin by folding the red frame, which will be the top of your shadow box.

Step 3:

Now glue the dark red paper layer (the front of the present stack) onto the front of the red frame. Align it with the bottom.

Step 4:

The next step is to fold the sides of the blue snowflake layer down.

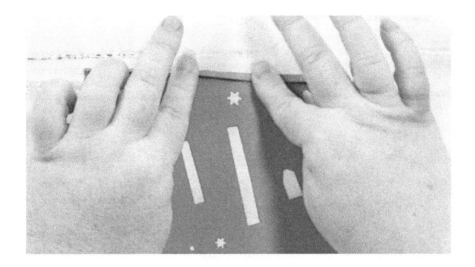

Step 5:

Glue the green Christmas tree onto the blue snowflake layer. Again, align the bottoms.

Step 6:

Then glue on the second layer of presents, the one with the gift card cut out.

Step 6:

Next, glue on all layers of the slider card. Bottom layer is yellow (it has the writing on it), followed by white, then blue, and finally red. Each of these layers align with the bottom of the yellow slider card.

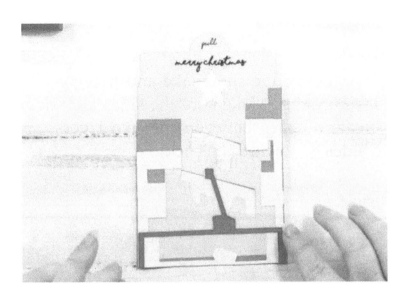

Step 7:

Fold up the sides of the green back layer.

Step 8:

Glue the sides of the snowflake-and-tree layer to the back layer's sides. Make sure the sides are folded so they create a space between the two layers (so the folded sides go toward the back).

Step 9:

Now glue the sides of the back layer inside the sides of the front frame, forming the shadow box.

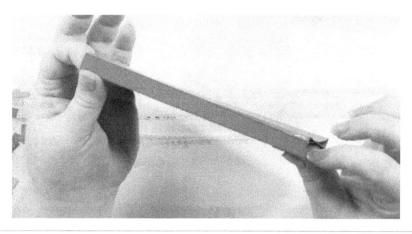

Step 10:

Insert your yellow slider card. If it is too tight to move freely, just trim a small amount off each side. Also make sure everything is working as expected. If any of your layers shifted during assembly, you may see other layers peeking through — you can fix this by snipping off the extra on layers as needed.

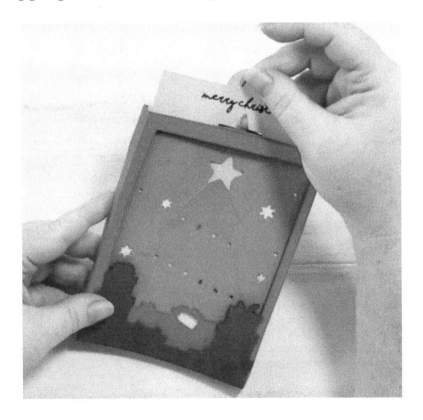

If you want to define the presents in the foreground, I included some color squares and rectangles to attach onto them. I recommend you use spray adhesive to attach these, as it will be cleaner than glue.

Tips

- You can write something on the gift tag, as I did. I wrote "Mom" as I plan to give this to my mother.
- It would be fun to decorate this Christmas tree more than I did. I can't have all the fun — I left it relatively undecorated so you decorate it as you saw fit. I would love to see you decorate it!!

Make Paint Chip Christmas Cards

I love receiving Christmas cards! So I really need to get myself back on the Christmas card bandwagon. I love that these paint chip Christmas cards are really easy to make! So if you're looking for an easy homemade Christmas card idea, this one is perfect! And come on, who doesn't love sparkly rhinestones!?

Materials

- Paint Chips
- **Card Stock**
- **Foam Glitter Stars**
- **Sticker Rhinestones**
- **Double Sided Tape**

Instructions

Step 1:

Cut out different sizes of triangles from the paint chip. Try to avoid the words wherever you can, but remember, you can always overlap the triangles to hide the writing if it bothers you.

Step 2:

You can stick to all green paint chips, or you can do multi-coloured trees. I looooooove colour, so I made mine all sorts of colours!

Step 3:

You can buy pre-made blank cards from the stationary store, but I just used some of my leftover card stock from when I made the **rolled paper hyacinth flowers** last spring. I loved how the stars really popped on this dark blue paper.

Step 4:

The paper was just regular 8.5" x 11" printer sized card stock (65 lbs). I cut the sheet in half once, scored it at the center and folded my cards.

Step 5:

I used double sided tape to attach the trees to the card.

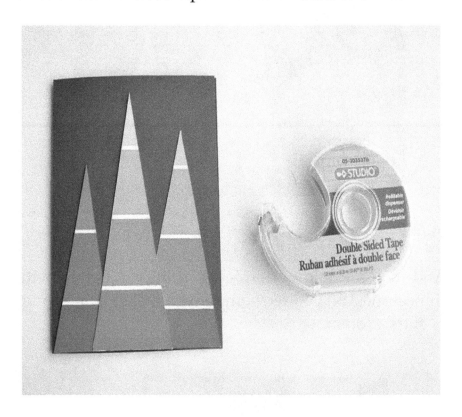

Step 6:

And then I added a foam glitter star sticker on top of the center tree.

Step 7:

And we all know that everything is better with rhinestones! So I added some silver sticker rhinestones as stars… or snow…

These paint chip Christmas cards are SO BEAUTIFUL! And they're super easy to make! You can choose any colours you like and personalize them for whoever you're sending them to. A single tree on the card looks gorgeous, or you can add a whole coloured forest like I did. Lots of options and really quick to put together!

Printed in the USA
CPSIA information can be obtained
at www.ICGtesting.com
CBHW032351031224
18411CB00030B/556